T0195950

THE SECRET SCIENCE OF MAKING 6 FIGURES WITH AIR AND LATEX

IT'S A SPIRITUAL THING

Balloon Me Pretty Balloon University

WestBow Press books may be ordered through booksellers or by contacting:

WestBow Press
A Division of Thomas Nelson & Zondervan
1663 Liberty Drive
Bloomington, IN 47403
www.westbowpress.com
844-714-3454

ISBN: 978-1-6642-4675-1 (sc)
ISBN: 978-1-6642-4676-8 (e)

Library of Congress Control Number: 2021920588

Print information available on the last page.

WestBow Press rev. date: 10/14/2021

WESTBOW
PRESS®
A DIVISION OF THOMAS NELSON
& ZONDERVAN

DEDICATION

To: J'nea, Jaila, Deshon, and Ja'Liyah:
Our future superheroes

"Build it and THEY will come"
- Unknown
Based on a quote from the movie Field of Dreams

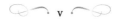

TABLE OF CONTENTS

FOREWORD

The words in this book go beyond words. It's a real solution for everyday people seeking truth, hope, guidance and motivation. It's knowledge that is centered with the essential components of life and liberty that have somehow been disposed of.

D. Sessions
Entrepreneur

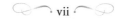

PREFACE

This book resulted from obedience to the Universe. "Tell the people who are seeking me the truth about hope, possibilities, manifestations, and how to create something out of absolutely nothing." The author is simply the messenger.

Wings were utilized in the logo of Balloon Me Pretty Balloon University because of what they represent. They symbolize the ability to escape; the freedom to fly over land, mountains, oceans, and problems

INTRODUCTION

We can all agree that anyone can manage to blow up and tie an air filled balloon, right? I'll even bet you $100 that we all either celebrate, or know someone who celebrates: holidays, birthdays, graduations, or weddings with balloons.

So, if the people of the universe collectively find an ocassion to celebrate every single day, why don't we have balloon stores on every corner in the same way that there are chuches or gas stations on every corner? In the same way that we need food or something higher than ourselves to believe in; there is a need for us human beings to celebrate! We need joy, we need togetherness, we need balloons so that our party doesn't resemble a meeting, yeah? Anytime we see balloons there's a good deed taking place in humanity.

And no, we shall not include your hypothetical cousin KeKe who watched 2 tutorials of balloon décor on google and swears on her mother that she will make your event look identical - free of charge. Now, we personally love cousin KeKe because that's how we get 99 percent of our last minute bookings. Everyone finds out the day before the event that her work looks nothing like the Pinetrest photos.

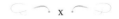

Some of us end up with cousin KeKe because maybe we assume the professionals charge too much if their talent and professionalism is something that we choose not to afford, maybe there isn't a local company. Perhaps everyone is legitimately booked.

Once the members of Balloon Me Pretty Ballon University realized that there really was an actual NEED for balloon décor; and that even if we tried, we couldn't service even 20% of the universe… we were commanded by the universe to help solve the problem! How magical would it be to invest into 1 course and have skills that allows you to service your own family, community, or friends for the rest of your life! Some pay $30,000 on traditional college tuition and can't even find a job afterwards in their field, or find that everything they learned was irrelevant as it pertains to real life work experience.

Yes, anyone can blow up a balloon or even declare they have a balloon business, but not everyone can consistantly make six figures with air and latex, or be blessed with opportunites to work with celebrities, be featured on mainstream television and radio as we have.

If you are interested in The Secret Science of Making 6 Figures with Air and Latex…Join us!

CHAPTER 1
WHAT'S IN A NAME

According to William Shakespeare's play Romeo and Juliet, "A rose by any other name would smell as sweet" could absolutely be 100 percent true, however, a business by any other name, could honestly smell like 10-day old, spoiled milk in the back seat of a car on a hot summer day.

Have you ever noticed that lots of small business owners in the event industry choose their own personal name for their business? There's absolutely nothing wrong with that on the surface. One of the secret sciences of Making 6 Figures with Air and Latex is realizing that although you may be a start-up or sole proprietorship doing everything on your own; you must give the illusion that is an entire force working with and for you.

Off the top of our heads do we really know the names of the people who own most of the major chains? Do we see their personal faces on their business logo? It's a wise decision to separate the business name from the person if it is a start-up business. A brand name such as: Nike, McDonalds, Balloon Me Pretty, Taco Bell, Wal-Mart is just that … a brand that's associated with the product and not the person. If Starbucks were called, Brandy's Coffee, do you think it would have the same worldwide ring to it? Create the illusion that you are a big brand. Study the greats and become greater or at least, match that same energy.

Notice that we said, match that same energy and not copy because we assure you that you will be going down a path in opposition of making 6 figures with air and latex. For the longest, McDonalds was the only food franchise that had two windows at the drive through. One to pay and the other to get your food order. Here within the last few years their seems to be more and more food chains also choosing to have two separate windows at the drive through. Seems like a brilliant, innocent idea on the surface to do it like McDonalds, right? Some ideas are better than yours, we get that.

Have you also noticed that these other food chains now regularly not use their second window? Do you know why? Because it simply does not work for the flow and efficiency of their business model.

When we first came up with the name Balloon Me Pretty, customers seemed to have the hardest time saying it because of the play on words. There was a clear vision in mind. We certainly thought of changing it initially, but the more time passed the more we noticed that people are calling in excited to say it. "I can't wait to be Balloon Me Prettied," they say now. They say it with so much respect that we blush about it. The vision that the creator gave us with the name was to cause things to be pretty with balloons. Strive not to do what the largest balloon store in the city does. Make the balloons pretty. Don't just hand someone a single helium filled balloon on a string.

That was the vision that the universe gave us. We have personally experienced a "company" within our own city that apparently loved our unique name so much that they used the same exact words and play on their business name as ours when they started their business. Mind you, they were aware of our existence. We reached out to the "company" and asked them if it were possible to change the first two words of their business name so that customers would not get confused when they googled us and end up with them because of the identical characters in the first two words.

This "company" told us that to them it was no different than Foot Action and Foot Locker and that they would not change the name to lessen the confusion with potential customers. We pleaded our case by stating that those were two major brands in the multi-million-dollar brackets, not two small businesses right around the corner from each other.

The moral of the story is… even if you admire someone for their work, understand that their work is their work and they are building a brand for themselves, therefore, you must build a brand for yourself. When coming up with a name for your business, search your own soul and spirit to see what the universe has specifically for you.

CHAPTER 2
THE INTANGIBLES

According to Oxford's dictionary: Morals: A person's standards of behavior or beliefs concerning what is and is not acceptable for them to. Integrity: The quality of being honest and having strong moral principles; moral uprightness; the state of being whole and undivided. Self-discipline: The ability to control one's feelings and overcome one's weaknesses; the ability to pursue what one thinks is right despite temptations to abandon it.

We have heard of these words, but do we comprehend them? How to be a "good" person wasn't a class that was taught in elementary or high school. Believe it or not, in some households, being a "good" person is irrelevant. Who are we when no one is watching? If there isn't a camera or documentation that exposes which person is lying or which person is telling the truth, where do you stand? Do we choose to control the things that are within our control to change, or do we validate excuses? Do we lie to ourselves about who we really are so that we don't have to change?

Here's a proverb for you - based on similar a quote from Sanvello.com: Cupid said to Death, "Why does everybody love me and hate you?" Death responded, "Because you are a beautiful lie, and I am the painful truth." – Unknown. Read that again. Some of us have really grown to love and accept lies. We don't care about the truth if it makes us feel uncomfortable or goes against our beliefs, or if it could cause us to lose something.

We can't speak for other businesses, but one of the secret sciences to making 6 figures with air and latex is choosing to have integrity, morals, ethics, self-discipline and accountability. When a customer pays you for a service, you must make sure you produce what they paid for. If you are supposed to be there at a certain time, then be there at that time. If they send you a sample of a picture that they want, and you tell them you can do it exactly that way, then do it. Sadly, it doesn't go without saying, but you cannot plagiarize other people's work and present it as your own.

Yes, some things happen that are not within our control. If you fail to show up on time, you must think of a way to accommodate the customer for that inconvenience. If you forget a full-blown event or mix your dates up, it's not even enough to just refund the customer. They trusted you for their special occasion and paid you for it out of all the other businesses in the world. They didn't pay you for the event just to get the money back. You must refund them and offer a free event, for example. Do what you say you are going to do. Period.

Now, on the flip side of this, please understand that some of your customers will not have ethics, morals, integrity, self-discipline or decency. This is the reason that we always encourage our students to keep everything in writing as much as possible, and more importantly, be extremely detailed in your invoices so that the customer is presented with what they are expected to receive and what services you are providing.

Some unethical human beings have taken the policies of some large chains and have illogically concluded that the customer is right even when the customer is legitimately in error. Perhaps they failed to read your cancellation policy, or failed to pay their balance, or accidently released their helium filled balloons prematurely and claimed you didn't give them the right amount. We totally watched a customer on camera accidently let go of her helium filled balloons, walk-back inside and allege that she was shorted one bag. She was embarrassed when we watched the footage together as she looked up to the heavens in slow motion watching the same bag in question drift away. Had she said it was an accident, there wouldn't have been any problems replacing her items.

Another secret science of making 6 figures with air and latex is comprehending that it is not enough to be human. You must be super-human when you are starting your own business. Your hours will be much longer than working a 9-5 but your bank account will also be longer – pick your poison. There will be days when you are exhausted or even sick, but a person that paid you $1500 for their child's 1st birthday party, I assure you, will not want to hear an excuse. You must pull from somewhere deep inside and make it happen.

CHAPTER 3
ABRACADABRA

Let me guess... you are thinking of a magician standing on a stage, pulling something out of a hat, am I right? Fine, let's think of it that way, except you are the magician. And instead of a rabbit, it's you that is working a job that you hate, it's you never having enough money to get passed your current circumstances, it's you, bored and rich wanting to be relatable to people, it's you that's feeling hopeless because you don't have the answers. You need to create something out of absolutely nothing. Abracadabra!

Most business that you can think of require lots of overhead, lots of capital and start-up costs, you need a good rental history to obtain a store-front, investors, and a business plan written by the prophets themselves. You know what you need to start your balloon business? You guessed it... air and latex! If you are breathing, welp... you are halfway there. Every dollar store or Walmart likely sells latex balloons for under $5 for at least 100. While we do not recommend using low quality balloons for your customers, it's a great place to get up the guts to start practicing. You will experience some loss of balloons while creating with them due to the low quality, but when you master your craft and start to utilize thicker, more expensive high-quality latex, as we do, then you won't have much to worry about. You will have good balloon babies.

I really can't think of many products for sale that will cost you less than $10 to make and you can charge

up to even $150 if you want for your hourly, your creativity, your time, your energy, blood, sweat and tears. Does anyone that you know think its unethical that a Picasso or Leonardo painting can get to the upwards of several hundreds of millions of dollars? If the Federal Government hasn't deemed it unethical that grass, wood, dirt and concrete in a decent neighborhood is several thousands of dollars, then how on earth can it be unethical for you to make a decent profit from something that you manifested from absolutely nothing?

One of our mottos at Balloon Me Pretty is "All Occasions, Every Event, any budget – We simply make it pretty". Now, does that mean that a customer calls and says they have $50 to spend toward décor, and we create whatever they want? Of course, not. It simply means that we will create something for them within their price range.

Another secret science of Making 6 Figures with Air and Latex for a small business is creating an atmosphere where you can service several customers in the same day. In this industry, lots of event vendors spend a lot of time dropping off and picking up items. We created a system where most of the décor that we do, the customer can keep or discard at their discretion. This system allows us to be available to do additional events rather than turn them down because of other events at the exact same time.

When you first start, your brain may tell you that you need a store-front to be successful. Believe it or not, although we have utilized a store-front, 99 percent of our customers never stepped foot in it. Establish a strong presence on social media and google. Be consistent to establish trust. I'll be honest, most of the fast-food, for example tastes kind of blah in my opinion, but they are consistent and dependable, and a little salt and pepper goes a long way.

Really meditate about how to utilize your marketing money. Some people go out and get these huge billboards. Unless it's a company that's established already, who really stops on the side of the freeway to jot down a new business phone number that they came across? I'll wait. Have you ever noticed that you could pass certain businesses for literal years and not even realize it's there until you google it because it's a service that you need in the area? Refrain from jumping on the train of what everyone else is doing. Yes, research and study to stay up to date with the latest trends but have a uniqueness about your business. Honestly, don't even start it until you decide why people should buy from you specifically. What do you offer, that they don't? If you can't think of anything, think some more. It will come to you.

CHAPTER 4
BUSINESS WITH MY PLEASURE PLEASE!

Pleasure: A feeling of happy satisfaction and enjoyment according to Oxford's dictionary. Now, it may make you feel super tingly and warm inside to do your best friends daughter's birthday free of charge. It's a nice thing to do. The materials don't cost you much, and it likely won't take you much time. She will love you for it, right? She's been having financial problems anyways, so this is certainly your good deed, yes?

Well, if that is your mentality, do me a huge favor and throw the whole book and business away right now. If your friend is suffering financially right now, the last thing on her agenda should be trying to throw a lavish birthday party. Be a great friend, for sure, but your business is separate from your heart. A business does not have feelings, but you do. You must separate the two - no matter how difficult it is for you to grasp. This is a major Secret Science to Making 6 Figures with Air and Latex.

Remember, you must conduct yourself like the larger brands if you ever want to become a larger brand. Study the greats and become greater, remember? When you go in to purchase groceries, to buy clothes, to purchase a car, to pay rent, does any of these businesses lower the price or offer you the services for free? Should they? No, otherwise they would be a charity and not a business.

"Maybe I should do a few free sponsorships to get my name out there and build my portfolio" You better not! Your beautiful work, your consistency, and integrity should speak for itself. If you don't respect that about your own business, no one else will. Now, after you get "rich" and you can afford to help the community with a few free events, that's a different story. After your friend has told you that she only has a $200 budget for you to work with, and you decide to add $25 of extra décor – there is no law against that because she told you the truth about her budget and respects your business by not expecting anything for free.

You will likely find that most of your support will come from strangers. It's really an odd thing, but I suppose it is like the scriptures; the son of God was simply not respected in his hometown so he had to travel to where the people would receive him.

Starting a business is not an easy task. There are many sacrifices that are involved outside of developing your own craft such as time management. Many people spend hours on top of hours being idle, watching television, scrolling on social media, partying, and having meaningless conversations.

What separates success and failure is almost always embedded in how a person spends their time. Unless you are studying the greats to become greater, you are doing yourself a disservice.

If you have ever watched any interviews of Michael Jackson, Kobe Bryant, Beyonce, Tom Brady, Tiger Woods, Serena and Venus Williams, or anyone else that you can think of who were considered great in their field, you will find that it wasn't this natural talent that they had. They studied more, they researched more, they stayed long hours, and consistently reinvented themselves. They are humble. They seek perfection within although the world thinks that they are already perfect.

Michael Jackson balloon décor created by
Balloon Me Pretty. He is better known as the King of Pop

If you are not where you want to be in life, you do not have time to be at every family gathering, and every social event. There are only 24 hours in a day, and you sleep, eat, drive, and restroom most of it. The Secret Science to Making 6 Figures with Air and Latex is to learn to not feel guilty about putting your financial freedom and prosperity goals at the forefront of your existence. If you are broke, it's simply not possible to have peace or be able to think straight concerning your true purpose in this realm.

We cannot reiterate it enough. You will have to work HARD. Very HARD, but smart. This mentality that we are giving you in this book is one without fail. If you are failing, it's because there's some aspect of it that you have decided to disregard. You can't afford to "do favors" right now. Work now so that when it's time for you to retire, you can retire! I have never understood it - when someone says they are retired but are working a job. Make it make sense.

Speaking of sense ... repeat after me, "I must utilize logic and ration at all times while conducting business." According to Oxford's dictionary: Logic: reasoning conducted or assessed according to strict principles of validity. Validity: the quality of being logically or factually sound; soundness or cogency. Illogical: lacking sense or clear sound reasoning.

Here's the thing; if you are an illogical person, you won't be able to discern whether your customer is making a baseless complaint, or whether the work produced looks nothing like the image that they sent you to duplicate. You have eyes to see just like they have eyes. You must be able to deal with truth even when it can cost you. If you are unethical, you will know deep inside that you are in the wrong, but still tell your customer that they are wrong. If you are illogical, you will tell yourself that your work and the image look identical although that is not the truth. In that case, you need help and that's why we offer mentorship because at that point it's a spiritual thing.

The battle is within regarding good, bad, and what perceptions we give ourselves. A lot of us are dealing with childhood trauma, dysfunction, abuse, self-esteem issues, ego, and bad habits. We must not project those issues on to our customers. The business and self are separate, remember? Business transactions are very simple. They ask for a service, you tell them you can provide the service that they asked for, they pay you for the service, you produce a receipt of said service detailing exactly what discussed, then you produce the service. The only time there are disagreements, or back and forth is either you have decided to be illogical, unethical, or immoral, or the customer has. Make sure you are always the logical one.

Décor created by Balloon Me Pretty

If for some reason, you never blow up a balloon in your entire life, do you see how these are principles and codes of ethics that you need for your existence regardless? If you are logical, of course you do. Sign up for mentorship as soon as possible if you are in opposition or don't feel a connection with these words.

CHAPTER 5
FAITH: THE KIND THAT WORKS!

There is an ancient proverb: Three spiritual men decide to worship a certain god. An oppressor tells them that if they don't worship him instead, he is going to throw them in a furnace and burn them to death. The spiritual men told the oppressors people that they were going to continue to worship their original god, and that they would continue to do so even if the original god did not come and save them.

This proverb really perplexed me for the longest time. Why would they continue to worship the original god if it didn't come rescue them? If the original god had the power and was worthy of being worshipped, wouldn't it be cruel of that god to just let them burn?

Through trials, tribulations, and resilience we realized that their will had become that of the god that they worshipped. They had the same mindset as it related to the world, they were not going to honor anything wicked or evil even if it killed their fleshly bodies.

The reality is, there is evil in this world, and things have been much harder than they should be at the hands of some selfish, demented entities. "They" have the power to manifest evil and hardship and you have the power to manifest righteousness and goodness. Eat from the tree of life and not the tree of good and evil. Hope ends, only when you give up; only when you declare a thing hopeless. According to the ancient prophets: Faith is a thing that is hoped for, and the evidence is not seen. Dr. Martin Luther King, Jr. once referenced it as being bold enough to keep walking up a staircase, keep taking steps, although you don't know where exactly it will lead you to.

Décor by Balloon Me Pretty

An additional Secret Science to Making 6 Figures with Air and Latex is receiving the Truth. Yes, there are some miracles, blessings, and mercy in this realm. But do not count on an invisible entity to fall out of the sky and create your business plan for you, or make phone calls for you, or start your website and create your business cards. The spirit gave you the freedom and choice to think and manifest.

Things will get hard sometimes. You will get frustrated at times. You will feel inadequate. You will have to fight yourself and tell your lower self to take a seat and be still! The spirit of fear, the spirit of anxiety, the spirit of hopelessness will absolutely come after you – yes, just like the boogie man. You must work hard and be dedicated to the cause of financial freedom and being of service.

You were not born in this realm to struggle to pay bills all your life. Air and Latex is your way out of mental and physical bondage if you take this book seriously. It was our way out, and that's why we decided to share it with you guys. We are not better than you, we are you.

Printed in the United States
by Baker & Taylor Publisher Services